Only Drunks and Children Tell the Truth

Only Drunks and Children Tell the Truth

Drew Hayden Taylor

Talonbooks
1998

Copyright © 1998 Drew Hayden Taylor
Published with the assistance of the Canada Council.

Talonbooks
#104—3100 Production Way
Burnaby, British Columbia, Canada V5A 4R4

Typeset in New Baskerville and printed and bound in Canada
by Hignell Printing.

First Printing: January 1998

Talonbooks are distributed in Canada by General Distribution
Services, 30 Lesmill Road, Don Mills, Ontario, Canada M3B
2T6; Tel.:(416)445-3333; Fax:(416)445-5967.

Talonbooks are distributed in the U. S. A. by General Distribution
Services Inc., 85 Rock River Drive, Suite 202, Buffalo, New York,
U.S.A. 14207-2170; Tel.:1-800-805-1083; Fax:1-800-481-6207.

Rights to produce *Only Drunks and Children Tell the Truth*,
in whole or in part, in any medium by any group, amateur or
professional, are retained by the author. Interested persons
are requested to apply to his agent: Janine Cheeseman,
Aurora Artists, 3 Charles Street West, Suite 207, Toronto,
Ontario, Canada, M4Y 1R4, Tel.:(416)929-2042, Fax:(416)922-
3061.

Canadian Cataloguing in Publication Data

Taylor, Drew Hayden, 1962-
    Only drunks and children tell the truth
    A play.
    ISBN 0-88922-384-X
    I. Title.
PS8589.A88O54 1998   C812'.54   C98-910021-9
PR9199.3.T35O54 1998

Acknowledgements

The birth and growth of a play sometimes involves what could be called an extended family—people who have, in one way or another, contributed something substantial and wonderful to its development. *Only Drunks and Children Tell the Truth* owes many thanks to many different people in this family.

First of all, this play couldn't have been written without the help and efforts of the people who worked on the original production of *Someday* (of which *Only Drunks and Children Tell the Truth* is a sequel of sorts.) This play is merely the second step in the journey, and the journey began with De-Ba-Jeh-Mu-Jig Theatre Group on Manitoulin Island. Many fabulous things have started there.

I am proud that several wonderful organizations and companies saw the potential of this play and aided me in that journey: I would like to thank all the wonderful people at Canadian Stage company who provided me with the opportunity to tell this story; The Banff Playwright's Colony where the actual birthing took place; New York Theatre Workshop and Native Voices–Illinois State University who allowed me to workshop this humble little play; and of course Native Earth Performing Arts who produced the play itself.

Personally, I would also like to confer my appreciation to the following people who gave me advice, support, or the opportunity to further explore and expand on what I hoped would be a good play: Megan Park, Randy Reinholz, Jean Bruce Scott, Carol Greyeyes, Columpa C. Bobb, Darrell Dennis, Kennetch Charlette and Elizabeth Theobald. Way to go gang!

But perhaps the biggest thank you I could possibly give would have to go to Larry Lewis. This play would not exist without Larry's intelligence, belief, and his ability to convince a man who knew nothing about theatre that perhaps he had a few things to say. It was Larry, wherever he may be, that taught me to ask, "Why not!"

And finally, a play of this subject matter owes a great debt to the people who have lived through their own stories of adoption and repatriation. The author only hopes that this play does their experiences justice.

On the cover:
"On a Moon Lit Nite"
mixed media, 1992, by George Littlechild
depicting, left to right, all his relatives:
1. Marquerite (Kanowatch) Littlechild (wife of Johnny)
2. Victor Littlechild (son of Johnny and Marquerite)
3. Peggy (Natuasis) Bull (wife of Chief Francis Bull)
4. Johnny Littlechild
5. Louisa Littlechild (daughter of Johnny and Marquerite)

Foreword

by Lee Maracle

There have been a number of Native playwrights plying their craft since Drew Hayden Taylor's first play hit the market, but Mr. Taylor was one of the first modern Native playwrights to meet with success. Being first gets you in front of an audience. What keeps you there is continuous growth—each work has to be better than the last. *Only Drunks and Children Tell the Truth* is the second play in a planned trilogy focussed on the "scoop up" phenomenon, continuing in some form to this day, in which a large number of Native children were removed from their homes, their communities, their culture, never to return. It is his finest piece of work to date.

Characters like those in *Only Drunks and Children Tell the Truth* can be found on any reserve: the sage, in the form of the not-so-old Tonto, full of understated humour; the clown, Rodney; the modern woman with strong historical roots, Barb; and her sister, the not-quite-as-likely Grace, the lawyer. This play is subtly layered: the conflict between Western values and Native values played out through the sisters, free of the usual didactic preaching; the conflict between Western ideology and Native wisdom, played out through the interaction between Tonto and Grace; and within each are the very specific conflicts that go on within the members of a family which has been torn apart through no fault of its own—the internal conflict of those besieged by external forces and dis-membered.

We all face the "invisible" enemy of circumstance, which has no face, no name. We refer to this enemy as "the system," "white society," "structural Racism," "institutionalized oppression." It is a sticky gossamer thin web of hesitation which wraps itself around each one of us, causing us to constantly question our ordinary lives. It creates a dichotomy within. On the one hand, Grace, the sister who was away, is a successful entertainment lawyer. On the other, she is childless, husbandless, living alone in an apartment in Toronto, her work having become her closest friend. Barb, the sister who stayed, works for the band, is typically connected to her community, tied to her family, has enjoyed her mother's upbringing, but something inside keeps her frustrated, unable to appreciate her life fully: the missing sister has never been absent from her mother's heart, mind, and spirit. The omnipresence of the missing Grace blinded the mother, re-shaped Barb, and blocked both mother and daughter from realizing a full relationship. All are strangely innocent in the creation of these many conflicts. All are extremely frustrated and unfulfilled by them.

Barb hesitates to call Grace during her mother's spiral down into death. Grace hesitates to return. Their mother, broken-hearted, has lost her zeal for living, hesitating to really look at her life free of the return of Grace. This failure to appreciate our lives, such as they are, arises of the blocks set in our paths by "systemic oppression." Sometimes shit happens. Mr. Taylor speaks to it in a very significant and extraordinary way: without the usual crassness, free of didacticism, proclamations, white society bashing. Nowhere in this wonderfully amusing, terribly tragic work does the "enemy" find a place on stage. The magic of good writing in my mind is to create the dramas of ordinary peoples' lives, to unfold them, and to keep the social conditions from which they arise solidly buried underneath in a way that jostles up the characters you have created. Mr. Taylor's *Only Drunks and Children Tell the Truth* does this very well. He does it in our own language. He does it in a way that is respectful of all the characters, men and women, and in a way that remains tender toward the society which has created the horror of loss.

This great care not to scrape the skin off white society creates an unusual hope for a future in what is otherwise a tragic condition. Hope is what we have so little of in our world. We have become bereft of hope, so bereft that many of our children are committing suicide. This play is so full of

8

life, beyond our oppressive conditions, without being at all shy of the necessity of pulling at the ugly knots this oppression creates: unravelling the "big ugly" and reweaving something else. *Only Drunks and Children Tell the Truth* is so rich in character, our characters, so native in the conjuring, that we can walk away renewed with hope for ourselves. Our selves, who in the long run are the only people who can change our lives.

The characters in *Only Drunks and Children Tell the Truth* are elegantly crafted, imbued with the sort of strength and flexibility that often is born among underclasses. This strength and flexibility is not conventionalized as heroic because it does not produce the sort of concrete results this product-oriented society expects of such conventions. For a western society struggling to produce Native works of art on stage, *Only Drunks and Children Tell the Truth* poses the challenge of showcasing the strength of Barb without losing her particular brand of sensitive flexibility.

Likewise with Grace, her strength lies in her knowing her boundary lines and in some sort of unspoken way retaining her understanding of her little sister growing up without her. There is an underlying yearning here, in the center of an imagined feeling which touches all the characters in one way or another, and Mr. Taylor's skill consists in never actually articulating this feeling, never directly addressing it, yet somehow holding it there for all to see.

In creating this piece of magic, this feeling, Mr. Taylor's *Only Drunks and Children Tell the Truth* gives you a glimpse of what it is to BE us. You are watching the yearning and the incompletion of all of us. His play does so poignantly, free of preaching, free of judgement about the other, and full of respect for us.

9

Introduction

Only Drunks and Children Tell the Truth got its start with an earlier play of mine called *Someday*, a play dealing with what Native people call the "scoop up," when Native kids were taken away for adoption. Too often with tragic results. I had never intended to write *Only Dunks and Children Tell the Truth*, assuming *Someday* would say it all for me. Evidently I was wrong.

I am a firm believer that sometimes a story is not quite finished. At the end of *Someday*, the ambiguity of the ending somehow felt right, but somewhere deep inside I wondered if this was truly the end of the Wabung saga? Does Janice really walk out on the family forever? What are the repercussions of this action? Does it have to be this way?

During the rehearsals for the first production of *Someday* in the fall of 1991, I was in the midst of a conversation with Larry Lewis, the director. At the end of *Someday*, Janice/Grace the adoptee, leaves her birth family and returns to Toronto in tears, unable to face all the emotions being forced to the surface. Larry asked me if I thought Janice/Grace would ever return. I responded that it would have to be something awfully important or persuasive to bring her back, knowing the kind of painful emotional experience she was going through. I off-handedly made a comment like, "Maybe a funeral or something. Maybe the mother dies."

It was then that I saw a familiar gleam in Larry's eyes, one that said his mind was already working out the possibilities feverishly. We spent the next hour talking about those possibilities. So *Only Drunks and Children Tell the Truth* was born in a messy kitchen, on a trailer located on the Wikwenikong Reserve, Manitoulin Island.

But as is my process, I let the idea ferment in my mind, along with all the other plays I was thinking about, for about a year and a half. As it was, I was in the middle of writing another play that was proving, shall we say, to be somewhat difficult. I decided to take a break and finally write *Only Drunks and Children Tell the Truth*. The first draft took me four and a half days.

In approaching this play, I didn't want to rehash all the arguments and points I had explored in *Someday*. Instead, I wanted fresh territory to develop and dramatize. Initially, the first play had been about the family learning their long lost daughter was coming home again after 35 years. It was the mother's and the family's story.

Only Drunks and Children Tell the Truth was Janice/Grace's story. *Someday* showed that you can't overcome 35 years in one hour. All things important and necessary take time. Repatriation, reunification, what ever you want to call it, takes commitment and resolve. And the road is not always smooth. I felt Janice wasn't as sympathetic in *Someday* as she could have been. It was time for Janice to have her day and face her demons. I was lucky enough to be a part of her journey. And poor Barb, the real rock of the family, needed to get some stuff off her chest too. She was in as much pain, in a different way, as Janice.

I also wanted this play to stand on its own, separate and complete. It would have been foolish of me to make *Only Drunks and Children Tell the Truth* dependent on *Someday*.

This play has been called a clash of wills, of cultures, of philosophies if you will. I think it's a story of two sisters finding each other. But as always, you will be the judges.

—*Drew Hayden Taylor*
Toronto, December, 1997

Only Drunks and Children Tell the Truth was first produced by Native Earth Performing Arts at the Native Canadian Centre in Toronto, Ontario on April 2, 1996, with the following cast and crew:

BARB ....Columpa C. Bobb

JANICE/GRACE ....Carol Greyeyes

RODNEY...Darrell Dennis

TONTO ....Kennetch Charlette

Directed by Elizabeth Theobald

Set/Lighting Designer ....Stephan Droege

Costume Designer.................................Kristen Fahrig

Sound Designer ....Denise Bolduc

Assistant Director* ....Shandra Spears

Production Manager............................J.K. Cuthbertson

Stage Manager ....Deborah Ratelle

* *Sponsored by the Canadian Native Arts Foundation.*

Cast of Characters

JANICE (GRACE) WIRTH, 36, sister taken for adoption, now living in Toronto.

BARB WABUNG, 24, sister living on the Reserve.

RODNEY, 25, Barb's boyfriend.

TONTO, 32, Rodney's brother.

Time

Late spring, early summer in 1992, approximately five months after the events described in *Someday*.

Location

The first act takes place in Janice Wirth's downtown condominium in Toronto. The second act moves to Barb Wabung's house in Otter Lake, a Reserve somewhere in central Ontario.

Act I

Scene One

Lights up on an upscale condo. Movie and theatrical posters adorn the walls, with the odd sprinkling of Native art. The place is empty. The quiet is broken by four loud and sharp knocks on the door. There is silence, then more knocks are head. Again, no response. A door bell rings repeatedly. Silence. Agitated whispering is heard on the other side of the door, a low decibel argument. Then the clicking of metal on metal, and jiggling of the door knob. The door opens to reveal TONTO on his knees in front of the lock. He has picked it.

TONTO:

> When in Toronto, do as the Torontonians do. Told you it wouldn't be hard.

> *He enters, followed by BARB and RODNEY.*

BARB:

> This is a bad idea, Tonto, this is breaking and entering.

TONTO:

> She's your sister, right? *(BARB nods)* It's not technically a B & E if it's your sister's place. It's a law, I think. Here's your jackknife back.

RODNEY:

> Cool, look at this city. I told you it was a killer view. You can almost see the Reserve from here.

TONTO:

> That's Lake Ontario. We're that direction.

RODNEY:

I didn't say our Reserve. I meant any Reserve. Six Nations must be....

TONTO:

That direction. Syracuse over there. You can almost see where Tyendinaga would be.

RODNEY:

Wow, Mohawks as far as the eye can see.

BARB:

Where do you think she is?

RODNEY:

Not at the Goodwill, that's for sure. Look at this apartment! Barb, when I grow up can I be an entertainment lawyer too?

BARB:

No wonder she didn't want to stay at our place. After seeing this apartment, I don't wanna stay at our place.

RODNEY:

Some of these movie posters are signed. Look, an autographed picture of Al Waxman. Is he still alive?

BARB:

Don't touch anything.

Without thinking, she picks up a piece of abstract sculpture.

BARB:

What is this?

RODNEY:

I think they call it art.

BARB:
How can you tell?

RODNEY:
It's in the middle of the table and it's not a bowl.

TONTO:
The woman's not as white as you thought. There's some damn good art up here. A Maxine Noel, an Odjig, a Roy Thomas.

RODNEY:
(*à la Star Trek*) Dammit Jim, I'm an Indian, not an art critic.

RODNEY disappears into the washroom.

BARB:
Think they're originals?

TONTO:
Well, they're definitely not prints. So either they're originals or great forgeries. And as much as I like Maxine's work, I don't think there's that great a market for fake Noel's. Someday, maybe.

RODNEY comes out of the bathroom.

RODNEY:
Barb, go look at her bathroom.

BARB:
I don't want to look at her bathroom.

RODNEY:
Trust me, go look at her bathroom.

Puzzled, BARB peaks into the bathroom.

BARB:
Wow!

RODNEY:
Didn't I tell you?

BARB:
I've never seen a bathroom like this. Tonto?

TONTO investigates.

TONTO:
What the hell is that?

BARB:
I don't want to know. It's like an amusement park in there.

RODNEY:
Hey, Barb. Take a look at this.

BARB:
What now?

RODNEY is standing in front of a photograph on a desk.

RODNEY:
See. She didn't forget.

BARB:
She still has it.

TONTO:
Still has what?

BARB:
The picture Mom gave her last Christmas. Of Dad holding her.

TONTO:
I'd forgotten how big your father was. How old was Grace there?

BARB:

About three months. The C.A.S. took her a couple months later.

RODNEY:

See Barb. It may not be a wasted trip.

BARB:

I miss that picture. Why didn't she return our calls? Couldn't she tell it was important?

TONTO:

I don't think she's been here for a while. This plant soil is very dry.

RODNEY:

You know, sometimes you're just too Indian.

TONTO:

Chi-meegwetch. And check her answering machine. Eleven calls. How many times did we call?

RODNEY:

Including the two this morning, ten all together.

BARB:

So she's not here. A three hour drive for nothing.

RODNEY:

So, what do you want to do? Hang out here and wait for her to get back, or do you want to head home?

BARB:

I'm tired, Rodney. I want to go home.

RODNEY:

You got it. Let's go.

They start moving toward the door.

TONTO:
Provided this godforsaken city hasn't towed my truck.

Suddenly, the rattle and click of keys in a lock is heard. The trio freeze, panic stricken like deer in headlights.

BARB:
Shit!

RODNEY:
Everybody hide!

They all scramble to find places to hide in the apartment. The door opens and JANICE/GRACE enters with her luggage. She looks tired and worn. Barely glancing at her apartment, she drops her bags and takes her coat off. She opens the closet to find TONTO.

TONTO:
Uh, hi....

JANICE screams.

TONTO:
It's okay! It's okay!

She goes into a martial arts position (Wendo) and punches him solidly. TONTO goes down in the closet, a flood of coats covering him in an avalanche.

JANICE:
(screaming) 911! 911!

TONTO crawls out of the closet in pain and half-conscious, only to have Janice start kicking him.

TONTO:
(in pain) Barb...!

BARB and RODNEY emerge from their hiding position.

BARB:
Grace! Take it easy. It's us!

JANICE:
  Barb? Rodney?

BARB:
  Hi Grace.

JANICE:
  What are you doing here? In my apartment?

BARB:
  We had to see you.

JANICE:
  How'd you get in here?

RODNEY:
  We, uh, snuck past the security guard and, well, Tonto
  picked your lock.

JANICE:
  Who picked my lock?

RODNEY:
  My brother, Tonto.

  *RODNEY gestures to TONTO who only now is getting up
  off the ground.*

TONTO:
  (still in pain) Hi. I spent a year working for a locksmith
  in Peterborough. It's quite easy once you know how
  they work.

JANICE:
  What are you all doing here? In my apartment?

BARB:
  Well, when you didn't return our messages....

JANICE:

What messages? Will someone tell me what's going on here?

BARB:

Grace, Mom passed away four days ago.

JANICE:

Anne..., oh Barb, I'm sorry. What happened?

BARB:

She went in her sleep.

JANICE:

Four days ago?

BARB:

The funeral was yesterday. I wanted you to be there.

JANICE:

Oh Barb, I'm so sorry. I've been away and....

BARB:

I think you should come back, and say good-bye, you know, to her.

JANICE:

Go back. *(realizing)* Go back?! Barb I can't.

BARB:

What do you mean you can't? You owe it to her.

JANICE:

I'm sorry about Anne, I really am. And I'll do what I can if you need any help. But going back...I can't.

BARB:

You have to go back. She's your Mother. Our Mother. I don't care if you just drive up, put some flowers down, say good-bye, hop back in and drive away afterwards.

RODNEY:
> You really should, Grace.

TONTO:
> It's the proper thing to do.

JANICE:
> Sorry, but I'll determine what's proper for me to do.
> Anne was a lovely lady....

BARB:
> Your biological mother.

JANICE:
> I knew her for one hour, that was all.

> *Beat.*

BARB:
> I don't believe you.

TONTO:
> What have you got against Otter Lake? That's where
> you come from, that's your people.

JANICE:
> My people live in London.

TONTO:
> No, your caretakers live in London, your family lives in
> Otter Lake.

JANICE:
> I love my parents.

TONTO:
> I'm sure you do. Look, I worked for a year as a counsel-
> lor at the Youth Centre. I met kids all the time, and
> adults, too, who were trapped between one culture and
> another. It can do weird things to some people. But I

found it can help if you have a sound understanding of where you come from, then you'll have a better understanding of where you're going. Got me?

JANICE:
That's really wonderful. *(to BARB)* I realize you're going through a rough time right now, Barb, but I really don't think it would be in anyone's best interest for me to go back to Otter Lake. The last time I left there, I was a mess. I'm still trying to get a hold of myself. I do not want to go through that again.

BARB:
Okay, you don't want to come home and say good-bye to the woman who gave birth to you. I'm not surprised, but I am disappointed. I hoped you'd been born with some of Mom's compassion.

JANICE:
Don't take this personally. It's me, not you. Now, if there's anything else I can do to help....

RODNEY:
Um yeah, as a matter of fact there is, Grace.

JANICE:
Please, my name is Janice.

RODNEY:
Okay, Janice. Um, we need a place to crash. Got any room?

BARB:
What? I don't want to stay here.

RODNEY:
Sweetheart, essence of my existence, we need some place to stay for the night. It'll be dark in an hour and Tonto can't drive because of his night-blindness....

BARB:

You have night-blindness?

TONTO:

It's a personal thing.

RODNEY:

I don't have my license since that little altercation with the O.P.P., for which I still think that breathalyzer was rigged. You don't like to drive on the highways. Kind of limits our alternatives.

BARB:

I don't want to stay here!

JANICE:

All of you? Here?

RODNEY:

We're house-broken.

BARB:

Listen to me, I don't want to stay here.

JANICE:

But Barb doesn't want to stay here.

RODNEY:

Listen, honey, do you want to walk home? Sleep in the truck or better yet, sleep on the streets? It's early spring so the chance of getting frost bite is practically non-existent.

BARB:

(to TONTO) How bad is your night-blindness?

RODNEY:

Trust me, it's very bad. We don't have a choice.

BARB:
Well....

RODNEY:
It's decided. Can we?

JANICE:
Well, I guess. You're all welcome to stay if you want. It's the least I can do.

BARB:
Can't get much more least than that.

RODNEY:
I think that's a 'yes.' *(to TONTO)* Shall we go get our stuff?

JANICE:
I'm supposed to be on vacation.

TONTO:
Why bother, you've got a natural tan.

RODNEY and TONTO walk to the door.

TONTO:
(to RODNEY) How long have I had night-blindness? Is it fatal?

RODNEY:
Shh!

They exit as the lights go down.

Scene Two

It is several hours later. JANICE is in the kitchen making coffee. BARB comes out of the bathroom drying her hands. They spot each other and there is an instant note of tension. BARB backtracks into the bathroom. There is silence for a moment.

JANICE:

You might as well come out of the bathroom. There's only so much you can do in there. I've made some coffee. Would you like some?

There is a pause before BARB comes out.

BARB:

Thank you.

JANICE:

How long do you think Rodney and Tonto—I can't believe I'm calling him that—will be?

BARB shrugs, unwilling to talk.

JANICE:

Is the bedroom fine?

BARB nods.

JANICE:

You're a little old to be giving me the silent treatment.

BARB:

Milk please.

JANICE:

That's a beginning.

BARB:

You wanna talk, okay then, I have a question for you. Why are you being so nice all of a sudden?

27

JANICE:

Fair enough. I suppose from your perspective I do deserve a bit of a cold shoulder. I wasn't exactly the warmest of hosts earlier. But you have to admit, it's a little unusual for the three of you to be waiting in my apartment. I just about had a heart attack.

BARB:

Back in Otter Lake, if somebody's not home, we wait inside.

JANICE:

This isn't Otter Lake. But I guess you had a valid reason for coming here. I understand that.

BARB:

How nice of you.

JANICE:

And I don't see any point for animosity between us. We are, as you keep pointing out, sisters of one nature or another. I'm not a bad person, Barb.

Again there is an awkward silence between them.

JANICE:

Do you come to Toronto often?

BARB:

Last time was Christmas.

JANICE:

It's quite the difference, isn't it?

BARB:

As Rodney says, "It's a nice place to visit but I wouldn't want to put a land claim on it."

JANICE:

He's got a very interesting sense of humour.

BARB:

He's a goof. But he's my goof. This is good coffee.

JANICE:

It's a Kenyan blend. Would you like some more?

BARB:

Yeah, that company makes good coffee I hear. I need a good jolt. Long car trips put me away.

JANICE:

It's decaffeinated.

BARB:

Decaffeinated?! Then what's the point? Got any real stuff.

JANICE:

You'd drink caffeinated coffee at this hour of the night?

BARB:

Yeah?

JANICE:

I'd be up all night. Not that it matters. I don't have any, what you might call "real stuff" in the apartment. Better warn you, no salt or butter either.

BARB:

Boy, we'll be outta here real early tomorrow. The more I talk to you, the more I realize there's nothing to talk about.

JANICE:

The subject of coffee is hardly the thing to base a relationship on.

BARB:

Sometimes it's all you got. Mom always wondered what kind of place you lived in. I always thought it would look something like this. Certainly better than our old house.

JANICE:

But that old house had character. This is just a condo.

BARB:

I know a lot of people who would trade some character for a condo like this. Nice art. Even some Native ones, I see. Tonto was impressed.

JANICE:

They were gifts.

BARB:

(to herself) Figures.

There is an awkward silence between the two.

JANICE:

So when do you think the boys will be back?

BARB:

In a little while I guess. Tonto wanted to see if there was a social tonight at the Native Centre. He's into things like that.

JANICE:

That's on Spadina right? Driven by it many times.

BARB:

Did you ever go in?

JANICE:

Never had the time. I notice I've picked up your habit of calling them boys. They must be on both sides of thirty.

BARB:

Yeah, but a boy is always a boy, even in the nursing home. I suspect Rodney will still be climbing trees in his wheel chair. Tonto won't be far behind him.

JANICE:

What a bizarre name. Tonto.

BARB:

Goes with his character.

JANICE:

What does he do?

BARB:

Anything and everything. Basically he survives off of various employment programs, apprenticeships, training incentives, stuff like that. He also drums a bit.

JANICE:

Oh, he's a musician. I used to date this jazz guitarist for a while. He....

BARB:

He's not exactly a musician. He sings traditional Ojibway songs.

JANICE:

Really? That must be interesting. He can make a living off of that?

BARB:

I think you're missing the point, dear sister.

JANICE:

(occupied) Sorry, didn't catch that.

BARB:

I was just thanking you again for taking us out to dinner. That was very nice of you....

JANICE:

...For a change. Is that what you were thinking?

BARB:

Maybe.

JANICE:

That always seems to be it, doesn't it? Always this, what would you call it, tension between us. All through dinner you barely said a word. It doesn't have to be this way, Barb. We could be friends.

BARB:

You're the one who doesn't want to say good-bye to our Mother. I'm sorry if that makes me a little sensitive. We shouldn't have come here. With all due respect, Miss Wirth, maybe we shouldn't stay here.

JANICE:

Little late for that, you're here now. Contrary to what you may believe, I have nothing against you or Otter Lake.

BARB:

You'd never know. You haven't even asked how the funeral went.

JANICE:

Fine, Barb, how did the funeral go?

BARB:

Fine as far as funerals go. Everyone was there, even the people she didn't get along with. Flowers everywhere, people. It was the first time I'd seen some of my uncles in suits since Dad died. Nothing quite like seeing a group of overweight middle aged men in mismatching, twenty year old suits all standing in a row.

JANICE:

Was it a traditional funeral?

BARB:
Yeah, Catholic.

JANICE:
I was raised Anglican.

There is another silence between them.

JANICE:
There's that awkwardness again.

BARB:
So much for the saying "Blood is thicker than water."
(pause) Nice view. Bet it cost a fortune.

JANICE:
What doesn't these days?

BARB:
True.

JANICE:
Your house has a nice view. I remember that beautiful
willow tree hanging over the lake. The view from your
kitchen window was quite special.

BARB:
You saw it in December. Now there are leaves on the
willow and the lake has thawed. Looks even better.
Except for the cottages.

JANICE:
What cottages?

BARB:
The band office has leased out land all along the
southern shore of the village to cottagers from the city.
They're everywhere, like a bad cold.

JANICE:
That's a little harsh.

BARB:
Sorry if I offended you. I didn't think you'd take it personally.

JANICE:
I didn't and we were talking about the house. Anne's house. Are you going to keep it, now that Anne has....

JANICE doesn't know how to finish the sentence.

BARB:
I don't know. It all hasn't sunk in yet. The house is a mess right now. Mom hired the boys to renovate the place with the money she won in that lottery. Add an extension, a sewing room, just off her bedroom. I don't know what I'll do with it when it's finished. I don't sew much. I don't even know what I'll do with Mom's room.

JANICE:
How are you holding up?

BARB:
I don't have a choice.

JANICE:
Everybody has a choice.

BARB:
Not me. When Dad died, I held the family together. When Paul died, I held the family together. I'm used to this now. I never had the luxury of being able to run away.

JANICE:
Most people would consider seeing their family for the first time in thirty-five years an emotional experience.

BARB:

Most people would have stayed for dinner. Most people would have called in six months. She loved you, you know. She did, even after you walked out on her on goddamned Christmas Eve. She still loved you. Thirty-five years of waiting and she was willing to wait some more.

JANICE:

I explained....

BARB:

Even when she cried, she still loved you. I knew you wouldn't be back but I couldn't tell her that. Her whole life had been built on hope, even after you left she still hoped. And as her daughter, I had to help keep that hope alive.

JANICE:

Barb please....

BARB:

Last March when she sent you a birthday card, your polite little thank you card said it all to her.

JANICE:

I was leaving on a business trip. I didn't have time....

BARB:

Neither did Mom. It was on her night table the morning I found her. You were always beside her. Always.

JANICE:

I had no control over that.

BARB:

Neither did I. I guess it's all Mom's fault then.

JANICE:

That's not fair.

BARB:

Surprise, surprise. I'm the one who failed classes in high school, who got drunk, rolled the car, who made her cry. But you were never there to disappoint her. You were the ideal, I was the reality.

JANICE:

I don't need this.

BARB:

Gonna run away again? Where this time? We're in your place. Or maybe your other family, your white family in London.

JANICE:

Leave them out of this. They have nothing to do with this.

BARB:

Nothing? Are we having the same conversation?! The government took you away from Mom and gave you to them. Did they ever once try to find your home, take you somewhere where there were Indians? Have you ever been to a Pow wow?

No answer.

BARB:

Just once I'd like to know what's going on in that beautified head of yours. You've always got those walls around you. Me and Mom spilled our guts to you but not the immaculate Grace.

JANICE:

I told you about my life, how I found you.

BARB:

You told us the facts. I don't know one damn thing about you, the person.

JANICE:

Oh, you're being ridiculous. Barb this is my home. You're welcome to stay here, spend the night, whatever, but I hope you'll do me the courtesy of respecting me in my own home.

BARB:

Like you said, it's your home. I wonder where those boys are?

JANICE:

Look behind you, in the corner.

JANICE points to a picture hanging by itself. BARB walks over to it and examines it.

JANICE:

I kept it. That picture means everything to me, even though I never knew him.

BARB:

Paul's picture. God, I can't get over how much you look like him.

JANICE:

Yes, I've been told that. I have two other brothers but it's not the same. They were born to the Wirth's. I know we don't see eye to eye, but I do acknowledge who you are and where you came from. I really wish you would do the same for me.

Suddenly the buzzer for the front door goes off. JANICE goes to answer.

JANICE:

That must be them. Hello.

RODNEY:

(voice over the buzzer intercom) Aye, Captain, two to beam up. Energize.

Janice buzzes them in.

JANICE:
Does he ever give up?

BARB:
Don't worry, tomorrow we'll be out of your life.

JANICE:
I wish we could be friends.

BARB:
I wish we could be sisters.

JANICE:
Friends are easier.

BARB:
Sisters are blood.

> *There is a knock and JANICE opens the door. The boys
> come in.*

RODNEY:
(à la Ricky Ricardo) Lucy, we're home. Boy, was it rough
at the club tonight! Where're my bongos?

TONTO:
Is that coffee I smell? I knew there was something
about this woman I liked.

BARB:
So did you make it to the Native Centre?

RODNEY:
Yeah, but judging by some of the people we met,
they're more off-center.

TONTO:

(fake laugh) Nobody was there so we took a look around downtown.

BARB:

You weren't hanging around in lingerie shops, again, were you?

RODNEY:

He wouldn't let me. But, Barb, look what we found.

RODNEY holds up a hardcover book.

BARB:

Not another one of your books. We got enough as it is.

RODNEY:

No, you'll like this one. It's the latest biography of Amelia Earhart.

BARB:

Really, let's see.

RODNEY hands it to BARB who looks it over excitedly.

TONTO:

We haven't had time to read it yet but they're always good for a hoot.

BARB:

Oh, cool, I love that picture. She looks so young.

TONTO:

I can't wait to show her.

JANICE:

Show who what?

BARB:

This one has her dying in Saipan, a prisoner of the Japanese, in 1937.

TONTO:
Give me a break, white people will find a conspiracy anywhere. Wait a minute, turn back. There's the plane. Ugly thing, eh?

RODNEY:
She never liked flying the Lockheed 10-E Electra, too clumsy.

JANICE:
Who are you talking about?

TONTO:
Amelia Earhart. Who'd you think? This coffee tastes funny.

BARB:
It's decaffeinated.

TONTO:
Yuck. The savages. How could they do that to an innocent little bean?

RODNEY:
Geez, when you think about it, another half an hour and she'd have made Howland Island.

JANICE:
Amelia Earhart, the pilot?

RODNEY:
You know another? My favorite theory of theirs is she was captured by aliens and forced to breed with Elvis and Jim Morrison to create television evangelists. That would explain a lot, wouldn't it?

JANICE:
But how come you know so much about her?

RODNEY:
> It's common knowledge back home.

JANICE:
> What, her fan club is located in Otter Lake?

BARB:
> Not quite. Remember the brown brick house about two
> hundred feet from our place?

JANICE:
> Yeah, I remember. I almost turned into that driveway
> by mistake.

BARB:
> That's where she lives. Just saw her yesterday at the
> funeral. *(to TONTO)* Maybe we should buy some regu-
> lar coffee.

TONTO:
> Definitely.

BARB:
> There's no salt or real butter either. If she tells me
> she's a vegetarian too....

JANICE:
> What is this? Some kind of joke?

BARB:
> What Joke?

JANICE:
> Amelia Earhart! In Otter Lake.

BARB:
> Oh that. Yeah, she and Mom used to be good friends.
> Used to baby sit me and Paul when we were young.

RODNEY:
Me too. Christ, she could swear better than any of us.

JANICE:
Amelia Earhart is dead.

BARB:
She's in her nineties but I wouldn't call her dead.

JANICE:
You're all not serious are you? Amelia Earhart? THE Amelia Earhart?!

RODNEY:
Except now she goes by the name Amy Hart. The cutest little, wrinkly, white woman you ever saw. Looks like one of those dried up apple dolls.

BARB:
It is Amelia Earhart, Grace.

JANICE:
Janice!

BARB:
Okay, Janice.

JANICE:
Amelia Earhart's been missing for over fifty years.

TONTO:
Fifty-five isn't it?

RODNEY:
Did the big belly flop July 3rd, 1937. Had her first bowl of corn soup in Otter Lake November 21st, 1937.

BARB:
It's true.

JANICE:

If this is all true, then this is fantastic! Incredible. How'd she get there?

TONTO:

That's another long story. You see....

JANICE:

And everybody in the village knows this? I mean about Amelia Earhart?

RODNEY:

Yeah, it's not as if it's a secret. Almost every kid from the Reserve has done some essay or project on her in school. After a while the teachers were getting suspicious so we had to make up a story about Indians having a special affinity for her, respecting her because she personifies the feminine presence of the eagle as it flies across Grandmother Moon. One guy even equated her with a legend of "the woman who circled Turtle Island" which he made up during lunch hour.

TONTO:

That was me. White people buy all this kind of stuff.

JANICE:

This is incredible! Amazing. The media will go crazy. This is the biggest story since....

BARB:

Now wait a minute. Don't get carried away.

JANICE:

But why? This could be....

BARB:

...Wrong. She doesn't want publicity. Her first husband was a publisher and she got sick of all the publicity. She came to Otter Lake to get away from it all.

JANICE:
> But you said everybody in the village knows.

RODNEY:
> Yeah, in the village. Because we're her family now. It's her secret but it's also ours.

TONTO:
> Telling other people would be like turning in a friend. No can do.

JANICE:
> Then why are you telling me.

BARB:
> Contrary to what you think, you are still family, whether you care or not.

JANICE:
> Then you're taking one hell of a risk.

RODNEY:
> Not really. So what if you tell somebody else, you'd look cute on the cover of the *National Enquirer*, but then it would just fade away.

JANICE:
> But I'm a respected lawyer. With connections. If I wanted....

BARB:
> Yeah, if you wanted. But I'm hoping you don't want to. No matter how long you've lived out here, I think you still have some Otter Lake in you.

JANICE:
> This is all so crazy.

RODNEY:

Yeah, but it kinda makes life interesting, don't you think?

BARB:

You're not going to tell anyone, are you?

JANICE:

I don't understand you. Not more than fifteen minutes ago you were criticizing me about Anne, now you entrust me with this "precious" secret of yours. What's the game?

BARB:

No game. This is who we are. Family, friends, we stick together.

RODNEY:

Except during band elections.

BARB:

Shut up, Rodney. At our place we always have people dropping in, visiting, calling, whatever. You, yourself, said our place felt like a home. Sorry, but this place doesn't feel like a home to me.

TONTO:

Yeah, bit cold to me too.

BARB:

The walls look so white my eyes hurt. Nobody has called, doesn't look like you get many visitors. You seem kinda alone here.

JANICE:

I have friends. I've been away for a while, remember?

BARB:

Alone?

JANICE:
    What's that got to do with anything?

BARB:
    Where we come from, you have to try, I mean really
    work at it, to be alone.

RODNEY:
    Yeah, and I've tried.

JANICE:
    I feel like I'm being cornered by the three of you. I
    have my life and you have yours. Why don't we just
    leave it at that.

BARB:
    There's always this barrier you put up. Rodney used to
    be that way, after Paul died.

RODNEY:
    But I'm much better now.

JANICE:
    The bottom line is I'm happy with my life. That's all
    that's important. It's getting late and I've had a long
    day. I would like to go to bed, if it's okay with you?

BARB:
    Your apartment.

TONTO:
    But it's not even eleven yet. I'm just waking up.

JANICE:
    (to BARB) You and Rodney have the guest room. It's
    already made up.

RODNEY:
    Great.

JANICE:

And I guess Tonto can have the couch.

TONTO:

(less enthusiastically) Great.

JANICE exits to bedroom.

RODNEY:

Come on, it will be just like when you lived with Marie. You spent half your nights on the couch anyway.

TONTO:

That couch was a lot warmer place, let me tell you, than Marie ever was. The things I do for you two.

RODNEY:

Yeah, like you care.

JANICE comes back into the room carrying blankets and a pillow. She puts them on the couch.

JANICE:

This should be okay. Anything else I can get you?

BARB:

A cure for night-blindness?

JANICE:

Help yourselves to the towels on the shelf in the bathroom if you want to shower in the morning.

RODNEY:

Oh look, her towels match. Come my little crab into the seafood salad of love.

BARB:

I hate it when you talk like that. See you in the morning. We're leaving bright and early.

RODNEY and BARB disappear into their bedroom.

RODNEY:
So, did you bring the trapeze?

The door closes leaving TONTO and JANICE alone for an awkward moment.

JANICE:
Well, if there's nothing else, I'll be off to bed.

TONTO:
What kind of bed do you have?

JANICE:
Pardon?

TONTO:
Your bed. What kind is it?

JANICE:
A Queen-size King Koil, why?

TONTO:
Awfully big bed. Awfully small couch.

JANICE:
Nice try, Tonto. You'll fit on the couch. Bigger and better men than you have slept there.

TONTO:
It was worth a try.

JANICE sees her luggage sitting by the front door and carries it to her bedroom.

TONTO:
Need any help carrying those big, heavy suitcases all the way to your room?

JANICE:
I got them here from B.C., another few feet won't kill me. Good night,...Tonto.

With her luggage, JANICE awkwardly walks to her room as TONTO watches.

TONTO:
Good night,...Kemosaabe.

Her door closes leaving TONTO on stage alone. He starts to make his bed on the couch.

TONTO:
The big beautiful city, a big beautiful Indian, a big beautiful bed. Now you'd think all those things would go together, wouldn't you?

He flops down on the couch.

TONTO:
We ain't through yet.

He pulls the blankets up over his head ending the scene.

Scene Three

TONTO, a sock draped over his eyes, wakes up the next morning to the sound of JANICE, in a house coat, making coffee and a snack for herself. He watches her for a moment.

JANICE:
I know you're watching me.

TONTO doesn't say anything.

JANICE:
Still want to play games, huh?

TONTO:
Since when is watching you a game. It's a free country, almost.

JANICE:
Do you want some coffee?

TONTO:
That would be good.

TONTO gets up off the couch and is dressed only in a T-shirt and underwear.

TONTO:
Here, try this.

TONTO tosses her a small package.

JANICE:
Hey, what's this? Coffee! Where'd you get this?

TONTO:
About 6:30 this morning the sun came streaming in through that big window of yours. Hard to sleep when there's a spot light on you.

JANICE:
I had to pay extra for a southern exposure.

TONTO:
When I worked construction for a year, I had to get up at that god forsaken hour. I swore never again. Except for sunrise ceremonies, of course. But even those are getting harder and harder to get up for. Anyway, I went to make coffee, found that decaf stuff of yours and thought "the hell with this." So, I went out and got some real, good stuff an hour ago.

JANICE examines the package closely, surprised.

JANICE:
I have travelled the world, shopped most of my life in every type of store possible, and I have never, ever, come across any coffee anywhere labelled "Extra-caffeinated." Where did you find this?

TONTO:
I worked in a coffee shop for half a year, so I know a little about coffee. Always remember, where there's a will, there's a way.

JANICE:
Is this the Otter Lake way?

TONTO:
If I wasn't afraid of needles, I'd take it with a syringe. We'll make an Indian of you yet.

JANICE:
Is that all it takes? Strong coffee?

TONTO:
That and a fine appreciation of good lookin' aboriginal men.

JANICE:
Well, I will say, you do have nice legs.

TONTO:
You should see the rest of me.

JANICE:
Thank you, but no. Your coffee will be ready in a few minutes.

TONTO:
I suppose I should get dressed.

JANICE:
Please.

TONTO:
An almost naked Indian scares you?

JANICE:
Just my reputation.

She points to the window. TONTO reacts with embarrassment and quickly tries to dress.

TONTO:
Holy mackerel, three million White people lookin' at me in my undies. Might start a riot.

JANICE:
The city of Toronto scare you, Tonto? Tonto. How'd did you ever get a name like Tonto?

TONTO:
It's a nickname, my real name is Eli Albert. Now given a choice between Eli Albert and Tonto, which do you think has more character?

JANICE:
I think Eli Albert is a nice name. But why Tonto?

TONTO:

My Dad used to work steel in the city a lot when I was a
kid. He'd always be going off to work for days at a time.
When I asked where he was, I was told "your Dad is in
Toronto," only I couldn't say Toronto, I kept pronounc-
ing it Tonto. The name kinda stuck.

JANICE:

I think that's sweet. Do you have a horse named Scout?

TONTO:

No, but I have a Bronco called The Anti-Christ.

JANICE:

You're a funny man.

TONTO:

How often do you work out?

JANICE:

Who? Me?

TONTO:

Yes, you. That shot you gave me yesterday was a professional one, if I ever felt one. And I'm ashamed to say
I've felt a few in my younger days. That punch went
right through me.

JANICE:

I took a Wendo course at my club. It's a type of self-
defense for women. I thought it might come in handy
some day.

TONTO:

You're lucky you didn't break your hand on my kidney
stones.

JANICE:

It wasn't that hard. Was it?

TONTO:
You could kiss it and make it better.

JANICE:
I could make it worse.

TONTO:
I'll settle for breakfast.

JANICE:
I'd better warn you, you eat at your own risk. I'm not much of a cook.

TONTO:
Well, what have you got?

JANICE:
Yogurt, I think....

TONTO:
Boy, this is really a fun house. I'll stick with the coffee. Is it ready yet?

JANICE:
Another few minutes.

TONTO picks up the bag of decaffeinated coffee.

TONTO:
I tried this decaf stuff once. Sort of like kissing a relative. Tastes the same but no spark.

He drops it in the garbage.

JANICE:
Hey, that's good coffee.

TONTO:
That's like buying beer with no alcohol.

JANICE:

Ah, one of those real men who doesn't drink non-alcohol beer.

TONTO:

One of those real men who doesn't drink beer, period.

JANICE:

I thought all Indian men drank.

TONTO:

I thought all women could cook.

JANICE:

Touché. Stereotypes everywhere. Sure you don't want the yogurt?

TONTO:

Pass.

JANICE:

If you don't mind me asking, why don't you drink?

TONTO:

My mother died of the stuff. That can sort of turn you off it.

JANICE:

Oh, I'm so sorry. I shouldn't have asked. Rodney never mentioned anything about that.

TONTO:

Why should he?

JANICE:

You're brothers, aren't you?

TONTO:

I was raised by his family after my Mother died. We sort of became brothers, I've lived with his family longer

than he has. I was there the day he was born. Looked
like a worm with legs.

JANICE:

You were adopted? Like me?

TONTO:

Yeah, except I stayed on the Reserve. Saw my real Dad
a lot when he was home. He worked in the city all the
time and couldn't look after me so the Stones took me
in.

JANICE:

That's Rodney's parents?

TONTO:

Rufus and Lillian Stone. Good people. Been with them
as long as I can remember. Actually, you're one of the
reasons I ended up with the Stones. God knows where
I'd be if it weren't for you and Anne.

JANICE:

Anne! What does Anne have to do with this?

TONTO:

It's too bad you never knew your Mother better. From
what I heard, she really kicked up a fuss after you were
taken, once she stopped being afraid of the authorities.
I guess taking your child away can really change that
fear to anger. Well, whatever, it worked. She rattled
some cages.

JANICE:

Yes, she told me.

TONTO:

But did she tell you that because of her fuss, the
Province decided to try a new program to foster Native
kids on the Reserve? I was an experiment. I was placed
with the Stones at the age of five and bang, here I am

twenty-seven years later, a fine human being. I hear
they do that kind of thing in a lot of places now.

JANICE:
You got to stay on the Reserve and I was sent away.

TONTO:
Yeah, but my case came eight years after you. A lot
changed in that time. And things are still changing.
Just think, Miss Wabung, you changed Native history.
Not a lot of people can say that. Your Mother saved my
butt. If it weren't for her, God knows where I'd be now.

JANICE:
Only eight years.... And my name is Wirth.

TONTO:
Wirth, Wabung, whatever. The truth is, we're kinda
related. Both being raised by other people. Sort of
brother and sister. And whatever Barb may say, you
look like you've got a good head on your shoulders.
I've seen some doozies out there. Next time you're
driving around this city, take a good look at those
people sleeping on the sidewalks. Our people. A lot of
them are you and me, sister. We were lucky.

JANICE:
And you got to see your Father.

TONTO:
Oh yeah, every month or so. It was all cool.

JANICE:
That must have been wonderful.

TONTO:
Ever been hugged by somebody who chews tobacco? I
heard your new parents were rich.

JANICE:
Yes.

TONTO:
There you go. Everybody got something.

JANICE:
(lost in thought) ...Something.

TONTO:
Rodney's cool for a brother. A little too book smart though. Sometimes you can't make head nor tail of what he's saying. He once spent an hour making a comparison of, get this, the colonization of North America based on the two sci-fi books: *The Martian Chronicles* and *Cats Cradle.* That guy needs to spend a little more time on this planet. He needs to know tradition.

JANICE:
And you can teach him this tradition?

TONTO:
I listen to the Elders. It's all really obvious. The trouble with Rodney is he thinks like a white person. His heart's Native but that brain of his needs a good tan.

JANICE:
Why do you say that?

TONTO:
There! Boom! You just said the magic word. The whole difference between Native people and White people can be summed up in that one, single three letter word. "Why?" White people are so preoccupied with why everything works. Why was the universe created? Why is the sky blue? Why do dogs drool when you ring a bell? "Why" is their altar of worship. Their whole civilization is based on finding out why everything does everything.

JANICE:
And Native people are different? What is your answer to why?

TONTO:
"Why not?" That's it. That's the answer. Why was the Universe created? Why not? Why do leopards have spots? Why not? Why do Indians and religious people play bingo? Why not? You keep asking why you should go home to Otter Lake. Instead of asking yourself 'why', you should try 'why not.'

JANICE:
Why should I listen to you?

TONTO:
Why not? Makes sense, huh?

JANICE:
I've been in therapy. It's not that easy.

TONTO:
People always want to make things difficult. The world was made a certain way. Accept it. It's like this whole concept White people have with, oh, what's that term..."finding your Inner Child." Now why would they want that? I mean children are great and all that, but seriously, would you want to start wetting the bed again?

JANICE:
I never wet the bed.

TONTO:
(uncomfortably) A lot of kids did. Anyway, moving on. That's the "White, Caucasian, let's go back to the beginning and try to get it right again" approach. Instead, they should do what Native people do, try to find their Inner Elder. It's a hell of a better pay off. A kid can only appreciate being young. An Elder can appreciate the young and the old, and everything in between. A Child would be afraid to go to Otter Lake. An Elder would interpret it as a necessary learning experience.

JANICE:

You make it all sound so easy. Flip a switch and your life is explained.

TONTO:

I didn't have to come here, you know. You're Barb's luggage and Rodney's too, I guess, by association.

JANICE:

Then why are you here?

TONTO:

Simple. On occasion, life can be a simple math problem. There are more reasons for me to be here, in this apartment than somewhere else. I had more to learn from coming to meet you, than staying at home. I hate Toronto but sometimes the pain can be worth it. Basically, the positive out-weighed the negative.

This sinks into JANICE for a moment.

JANICE:

You have some interesting theories.

TONTO:

It's more than that. It's practice. I never preach anything I don't practice.

JANICE:

I'll remember that. You're an interesting fellow. Certainly not what you seem to be. A bit of a closet philosopher, perhaps?

TONTO:

Nah, as Rodney would say, I came out of the closet years ago. The philosophy closet that is. So are we gonna get breakfast?

JANICE:

Oh yes, I suppose we should. There's a charming place just down the street.

TONTO:
Sounds great to me. Let's go.

JANICE:
I think we should wait for the others. They might want to eat too.

TONTO:
Good point. Then let's get them up. Leave it to me.

TONTO marches over to the door and bangs heavily on it.

TONTO:
Okay you two. Up and at 'em. I'm hungry.

There is some mumbling and giggling in the other room and RODNEY shouts out.

RODNEY:
Okay, we'll be out in...five minutes.

BARB:
No, ten minutes.

RODNEY:
Yeah, yeah, ten minutes.

TONTO:
I'll handle this.

TONTO opens the door and barges in. There is a scream, then TONTO comes out dragging the blankets.

TONTO:
If I'm not getting it, nobody is. And I said I'm hungry. Move it. *(to JANICE)* What are big brothers for?

RODNEY stumbles out as he does up his jeans. He's angry.

RODNEY:
Do you mind? We were…busy.

TONTO:
You've got the rest of your life for that. We only have this morning to eat. It's a long drive back, remember.

JANICE:
Um, Rodney, we're going to breakfast down the street. You better dress for it.

TONTO:
You heard the lady.

RODNEY:
And to think I could have been an only child.

BARB comes out of the bedroom, also angry, and buttoning up her shirt.

BARB:
There you are.

TONTO:
You still may become an only child.

He hides behind JANICE.

TONTO:
Now Barb….

BARB:
Come here Tonto….

TONTO:
Barb, I was just a little hungry, that's all. Rodney?

RODNEY:
You're on your own, pal.

TONTO:
    Janice?

JANICE:
    I don't believe you three. Barb, take it easy. He was just joking around.

BARB:
    You're defending him! What did you do to her?

TONTO:
    Nothing!

JANICE:
    Everybody just calm down and take it easy, okay?

BARB:
    (to TONTO) You're living on borrowed time, buddy.

TONTO:
    Respect your elders, I'm older than you remember.

BARB:
    Then act it.

TONTO:
    I got real coffee.

        Pause.

BARB:
    You're forgiven.

RODNEY:
    Ah, coffee has charms to soothe the savage breast.

TONTO:
    Help yourself.

        RODNEY pours himself a cup of coffee.

RODNEY:

I love the smell of Nabob in the morning. Somebody mention something about breakfast?

TONTO:

Yeah, down the street.

JANICE:

When you're all ready we'll grab breakfast before we leave.

BARB:

What do you mean "we leave"?

JANICE:

I mean we. I changed my mind. I'm going with you.

BARB:

(to TONTO) What *did* you do to her?

JANICE:

Now if you'll excuse me, I'll get my things.

JANICE exits the room to get her things.

BARB:

(repeating the words) She's coming back with us? She's coming back with us?!

RODNEY and TONTO give each other the thumbs up signal.

Lights go down.

End of Act I

Act II

Scene One

The scene opens on the Otter Lake Reserve in an old, lived-in house. There is a missing wall at one end due to ongoing renovations. The house is empty until JANICE appears in the doorway. Alone and silent. The implications and memories of this house flood her. Finally she enters and slowly glides through the room, taking in the texture and atmosphere of the house she was born in. She stops at a large photograph of Anne and Barb. Her solitude is interrupted when RODNEY, in full song, enters carrying a duffel bag, odds and ends, and the book about Amelia Earhart.

RODNEY:
"Country roads, take me home, to the place I was born, Otter Lake, mountain Mama, take me home, country roads...." Thank you. Thank you. Please, hold your applause.

JANICE:
Was that song for my benefit?

RODNEY:
I don't do benefits.

JANICE:
Do you have an off button? Travelling in a car with you for three hours is like a cheap trip to Vegas. How does Barb put up with all your high energy all the time?

RODNEY:

Best recipe for a solid relationship: good food, good sex, good times. Not necessarily in that order. I do what I can to keep my little Indian princess happy. I give her the surreal, she gives me the real. Not conventional, I'm sure, but it works for us.

BARB enters.

BARB:

Boy, you really made Tonto's day by letting him park your Saab.

JANICE:

He seemed so taken with it.

RODNEY:

He spent a year as a mechanic, so he has a fondness for good quality cars.

JANICE:

He will be careful with it, won't he?

RODNEY:

He'll treat it like his own. I think he's in love. You're the first women he's ever met with a car better than his.

JANICE:

I don't go anywhere without my car.

RODNEY:

Neither does he. Which makes sense considering there's no place to go in, or around, Otter Lake without a car.

BARB:

The place hasn't changed much, has it?

JANICE:
The refrigerator was over there, wasn't it?

BARB:
Good memory. Mom moved it until the renovations are finished. Do you want to go to the graveyard now?

JANICE:
Not right now.

BARB:
You're not backing out, are you?

JANICE:
Barb, I just got here. I need to rest and adjust first. Not everybody runs on your timetable.

BARB:
(to RODNEY) Did we bring everything in?

RODNEY:
Yep.

BARB:
Anybody want anything to drink?

JANICE:
Ah yes, the quintessential pot of tea. I remember that from my last trip. Do you have any herbal tea?

BARB:
What do you think?

JANICE:
Of course not. I'll pass for now.

BARB:
Think meat and potatoes. That's us. I was nineteen years old before I had Lasagna. Twenty-two before I had a stir fry.

RODNEY:

This is sort of like *Dynasty* meets *The Dukes of Hazzard.*

TONTO enters, holding a car part.

TONTO:

Hey Grace....

JANICE:

Please, my name is....

JANICE and BARB and RODNEY and TONTO:

Janice.

TONTO:

Okay, Janice. Do you know what this is?

JANICE:

It looks like a car part!

TONTO:

It is but I've never seen anything like it. I got it out of your car. I don't know what it does. I was hoping you would know.

JANICE:

You took it out of my car?! Why did you do that?

TONTO:

Why not?

BARB:

Tonto, put it back.

TONTO:

I intend to. Just curious, that's all.

BARB:

Rodney, go help him.

TONTO:
    It's not that difficult.

BARB:
    Then go work on the house. There's a hell of a draft
    coming through the wall over there. Do something.
    Just get out.

RODNEY:
    Barb, what are you trying to say?

TONTO:
    Hey, little brother, let's go. I think there's something
    happening here.

RODNEY:
    Oh, women stuff. Okay then, let's go out and do some-
    thing manly. Bet I can spit farther than you can.

TONTO:
    Gra...Janice, if you want, I can take you up to the
    graveyard when you want.

JANICE:
    Thank you. Maybe later. After you put the part back.

TONTO:
    Okay.

    He and RODNEY exit.

JANICE:
    Tonto is so different from Rodney. Hard to believe they
    consider themselves brothers.

BARB:
    I know but Rodney has his serious side. He doesn't like
    to show it but it's there. Last Christmas when you left,
    Mom was in a terrible state. I'm not telling you this to
    make you feel guilty or anything, just Mom sort of went

69

to pieces. Goddamn, if Rodney wasn't in here trying twice as hard to make us laugh. At first we weren't in the mood, but I'll say this for the guy, he's quite infectious. Normally Rodney doesn't like that sort of family thing. After Paul died, they were really close, he couldn't handle the heavy emotional stuff, and tended to run away from it. But not that time. He stayed the weekend, did most of the cooking, chopped the wood. Everything. While I looked after Mom.

JANICE:
I'm glad somebody was there for you.

BARB:
So am I. Enough of this depressing stuff. Like I said earlier, wanna drink? And I'm not talking about tea?

BARB pulls out a case of beer and drops it with a thump on the table in front of JANICE.

BARB:
Have a drink.

JANICE:
I'm really not a beer drinker.

BARB opens a cupboard door revealing rows of liquor bottles.

BARB:
Fair enough. How about some Vodka, Rye, Rum, Gin or Tequila?

JANICE:
No, thank you. If I was in the mood for a drink, I would prefer a white wine.

BARB:
Figures you'd prefer white.

BARB grabs a bottle of white wine out of another cup-board and puts it on the table.

JANICE:
Barb, I don't mean this to sound critical but do you have, by any chance, a drinking problem?

BARB:
With a mother like Anne, I don't think so. The only liquor she would allow in this house was in Rum cakes.

JANICE:
Then why...?

BARB:
Later. This bottle fine?

JANICE:
I'm partial to Chardonnay.

BARB pulls another bottle out and puts it on the table in front of JANICE.

BARB:
French?

JANICE:
Wonderful.

BARB:
Any particular year you're fond of?

JANICE:
Barb, it's barely four o'clock and I don't feel like a drink.

BARB:
Oh, yes, you do.

BARB finds a corkscrew and attacks the wine bottle.

JANICE:
What are you up to?

BARB:
I bought all this stuff the other day, hoping we could talk you into coming up here.

JANICE:
Why?

BARB:
Because, big sister, I want to get to know you.

JANICE:
You can do that by getting me drunk? Isn't that a little cliché?

BARB:
Mom had a saying, and I think it's true: only drunks and children tell the truth. I want the truth, and you're a little tall to be a child. So, drink up.

BARB hands JANICE her mug of wine. JANICE reads the mug.

JANICE:
"Today is the first day of the rest of your life."

JANICE reads the opposite side of the mug.

JANICE:
"Provided you're not dead already." That's uplifting.

BARB:
A birthday present from Rodney. Sorry, no fancy wine glasses, but I do have some Tupperware, if you....

JANICE:
This will be fine. You actually brought me up here to get drunk?

BARB:
And say good-bye to Mom.

BARB, with a physical gesture, urges her to drink.

JANICE:
I'm having a problem understanding this. If Anne was against drinking in this house, then....

BARB:
...Why all this? Mom used to say, "God works in mysterious ways, and so does Barb." Why should the mystery stop with Mom's being gone? You know, you've really got to quit asking why. Especially when it comes to hospitality.

JANICE:
Please, I've had this lecture.

BARB:
Tonto?

JANICE:
The same. Quite an interesting man. Has he ever been to university?

BARB:
He painted the residences at Trent University one summer but that's about it. That's our Tonto.

JANICE:
I bet if he really applied himself...Rodney too.

BARB:
Don't underestimate Rodney. He's taken more university and college courses than there are pearls in your necklace. They're both kind of the same. They just learn what they want to know, then move on.

JANICE:

Some would consider that a waste of time and money.

BARB:

Not everybody wants to be a lawyer. Some people are happy being who they are.

JANICE:

What if who they are is a lawyer.

BARB:

Then God help them. Cheers.

> *BARB forcibly toasts with JANICE, and they drink, though JANICE is still unsure. BARB refills the slightly drained cup and she continues to do this at every opportunity.*

BARB:

Lighten up there, Janice-Grace. Sit down, put your feet up, suck it back. Make yourself at home.

JANICE:

You do this often?

BARB:

Nah, can't drink like I used to, not like when I was a kid. Takes days to recover now. And besides, Rodney acts the fool enough for both of us, the entire Reserve, maybe the country.

JANICE:

I see.

BARB:

This is an example of what I mean about me spilling everything but not you. You just sit there so prim and proper, keeping quiet while the world around you blabs on.

JANICE:

If you remember correctly, the last time I was here, I
left in tears. I'd hardly call that prim and proper.

BARB:

Yeah, but you didn't tell us why you were crying.

JANICE:

Wasn't it obvious?

BARB:

Maybe, maybe not. The point is you ran away when you
started crying, like it was a weakness. Families were
created for weaknesses.

JANICE:

Barb the philosopher.

BARB:

Barb the realist.

JANICE:

Reality is what you make it.

BARB:

No, reality is what it makes of you. Oh my God, I sound
like Tonto.

JANICE:

Can we do something about all this liquor? I feel like a
drunken businessman will try to pick me up any
moment.

BARB:

You got it.

They both get up and move the liquor to the counter.

JANICE:

So what is the case with you and Rodney? Is he going to move in with you now?

BARB:

He's been here almost constantly since Mom...you know. He's been very good. Even been sleeping on the couch at nights. When Mom was alive, we had too much respect to do anything in the house. Then, well...last night at your place was the first time we'd slept together since it happened.

JANICE:

Remind me to wash those sheets. You haven't answered my question. Is Rodney going to be moving in with you?

BARB:

Why do you want to know?

JANICE:

Discovery is a two way street.

Beat.

BARB:

I don't know what we're gonna do. Maybe we'll build a new house and shut this one down. It's that room.

JANICE:

What room?

BARB:

Mom's room. I can't go in there. Even after four days it makes me feel too weird. I just hope it doesn't turn into one of those dust covered shrines weird old people have.

JANICE:
Tell me about her. About Anne. I knew her for less than an hour. I want to know more.

BARB goes to the doorway of Anne's room.

BARB:
Let me show you something.

BARB hovers in the doorway

BARB:
I can't go in. Grace, you'll have to.

JANICE:
For the thousandth time, my name is....

BARB:
(pointing) Right there. That package. Get it.

BARB returns to the table and JANICE enters the room and returns carrying a wrapped box.

JANICE:
What's this?

BARB:
Your birthday present from March. Mom was hoping some day you'd show up and she could give it to you in person. That's the kind of mother she was. And, like everything else, that responsibility now falls to me.

JANICE:
I don't like that attitude. Quit making me out to be a villain. I'm not.

BARB:
Are you going to open the present or not?

JANICE:
In a minute.

BARB:

"In a minute!?" Your first present from your birth mother and you say "in a minute?!"

JANICE:

These are unfamiliar waters for me. I want to take it slow and calm. That's why I left last time. It was too much too soon. I crumbled. Thirty-five years stuffed into an hour.

BARB:

We did a little crumbling ourselves.

JANICE:

Was she buried beside Paul?

BARB:

Of course. And Dad. The funeral even made the local papers. Wanna see?

JANICE:

Please.

BARB:

Most of the Reserve came, and quite a few from town. The only time she ever made the papers: when she won that lottery money, and when she died.

JANICE:

I recognize the Church from the drive in. I take it she was well respected.

BARB:

Respect isn't the word. Mom was...Mom. Everybody knew her.

JANICE:

Who's that old woman in the wheelchair?

BARB:
Oh, that's Amy, Amelia Earhart.

JANICE:
Not that again. I'm sorry I don't buy it.

BARB:
You don't have to buy it. Look out the window. Go
ahead.

Hesitant but defiant, JANICE goes to the window.

BARB:
See the brown brick house way down there?

JANICE:
Yeah?

BARB:
That's where she lives.

Beat.

JANICE:
Amelia Earhart, who has been missing for over fifty-five
years, the focus of one of the greatest, continuous
searches in history, lives in a small brown brick build-
ing on the Otter Lake Reserve in Ontario, Canada?

BARB:
Why not? Elvis could be a making Lacrosse sticks in Six
Nations for all we know.

JANICE:
If that is her, how the hell did she get here?

BARB:
Easy. Her plane went down in the ocean. The plane
sank in eight minutes with her navigator. She was
picked up the next day by a Filipino fishing boat.
Nobody spoke English and they didn't know who she

was. Two weeks later she arrives at some small fishing port in the Philippines, travelling, what's that word, incognito. All that time in the sun had made her very dark. She dyed her hair black. Bought passage on a boat to the States. A month later she's here. Simple.

JANICE:

But why? It makes no sense. What's the motivation. Why here? This little out-of-the-way jerk water Indian Reserve in the middle of nowhere.

BARB:

She was in love. We had a lot of iron workers come from around here. A lot worked in New York for months at a time. She met Adam Williams, the man who owned that house.

JANICE:

But wasn't she married?

BARB:

To some publisher-type guy, but it wasn't much of a marriage.

JANICE:

So you're telling me Amelia Earhart ran off with an Indian iron worker. Just like that?

BARB:

You haven't seen our iron workers. It was a perfect opportunity. She was supposed to be dead. She was tired of all the publicity and headaches. Hello Otter Lake. She liked what this place had to offer. It became home.

JANICE:

This is too weird.

BARB:

This is Otter Lake.

JANICE:
I still don't believe you.

BARB:
Wanna meet her?

JANICE:
What?

BARB:
Wanna meet her? I know she's home right now. We could go visit. I know she wants to meet you. Mom told her all about you.

JANICE:
I don't know....

BARB:
Afraid of the truth? It is Amelia Earhart. And I'm going to prove it to you.

BARB goes to the window and yells.

BARB:
Hey you two, come here. *(to JANICE)* Get your shoes on.

JANICE:
Do you think we should?

BARB:
Definitely.

The boys enter.

RODNEY:
You yelled, sweetness?

BARB:
I want you or him to drive us down to Amy's, okay sweetie?

TONTO:

Sweetie? Have you been drinking?

The boys see all the liquor.

TONTO:

Holy mackerel! Where'd all that come from?

RODNEY:

Must be a Chief's Convention in town.

BARB:

You leave that stuff alone. That's for Grace and me.

TONTO:

You got a stomach pump to go with it?

BARB:

Just drive us, okay? We'll take care of the rest. Let's go.

BARB and JANICE get up to leave.

JANICE:

Oh, Barb, I'm out of wine.

BARB:

No problem, got more, lots more. It ain't a
Chardonnay, but around here we have a saying:
beggars can't be choosers. You'll just have to force
down this Beaujolais.

JANICE:

Philistines. No more Chardonnay. I'm going to
complain to the manager.

BARB:

Rodney, grab me a couple beers. I'm running low.

The women walk out giggling.

TONTO:

What the hell was all that?

RODNEY:

Be afraid, be very afraid.

BARB:

(off stage) Rodney!

RODNEY:

Coming dear.

RODNEY grabs some beers.

TONTO:

You know what's going on, don't you?

RODNEY:

Relax, things are going smoothly. Just as I planned.

TONTO:

Any smoother they'll be unconscious.

Scene Two

It is approximately an hour later and a bit darker. The door opens and TONTO enters, supporting JANICE who is extremely drunk.

TONTO:
Easy going. Right in here.

JANICE:
Hey, I've been here before. Thirty-six years ago.

She bursts out laughing drunkenly.

TONTO:
Yeah, yeah, you're hilarious.

RODNEY and BARB enter in the same state.

BARB:
I love you, Rodney.

RODNEY:
So do I.

The two men dump them at the seats.

TONTO:
What now?

JANICE:
Barb, wine.

BARB:
(whining) Okay.

They both burst out laughing.

TONTO:
You realize this was one of the reasons I gave up drinking.

BARB looks up at the boys.

BARB:
Are you two still here?

RODNEY:
Yeah.

BARB:
Why?

JANICE:
Why not?

JANICE laughs at her own joke.

BARB:
Girls night out. Out! *(to Tonto)* You too.

TONTO:
Maybe, like, you two should cut down a bit.

JANICE:
It's Barb's idea. We're celebrating Anne.

TONTO:
Yeah, well, I don't think it's right.

BARB:
Just like a man. Just when you're having a good time, they go and pull out.

Confused, TONTO looks at RODNEY.

RODNEY:
Hey, she's not talking about me. You think maybe they're bonding a little too much?

TONTO:
Was that your idea?

RODNEY:
My idea was to get them together alone, by themselves somewhere.

TONTO:
Maybe they can share a room at the detox centre.

BARB:
OUT!

They exit quickly.

BARB:
Okay, straighten up. It's time to get serious.

JANICE:
Well, for two people who don't drink much, we're sure doing okay.

BARB:
Rodney is so cute, isn't he?

JANICE:
Yep, cute, that's the word I was thinking. Cute. Cute Rodney. Rodney the cute. Sir Rodney the Cute. Barb, what's he like in bed? Is he any good?

BARB:
Let's find out. *(yelling)* Hey Rodney, come here.

RODNEY sticks his head in the doorway.

BARB:
Grace wants to know if you're any good in bed?

Beat.

RODNEY:
Um...Uh...

For once RODNEY has no snappy retort. He quietly disappears back outside. They burst out laughing again.

JANICE:

He is cute. Want another one?

BARB:

You betcha. I thought you didn't drink beer.

JANICE:

Like you said, "beggars can't be choosers."

BARB:

I haven't done this in years.

JANICE:

Barb, do you think it was proper for us to go over to Amy's like this? In this condition I mean?

BARB:

Oh, Amy could throw them back with the best of them. If anything I think she found us funny. I wonder why? So what did you think of our little Amy Hart?

JANICE:

My Lord Christ, you were right. That is her. I can't believe it!

BARB:

Believe it. And I can't believe you offered to represent her as her lawyer! That is so tacky.

JANICE:

I know, I know. It just sort of popped out. The lawyer runs deep, I guess. What was that she said to me in that language.

BARB:

It's called Annishnawbe, Ojibway for Christ's sake. Will you get these things straight? This isn't kindergarten.

JANICE:

Amelia Earhart speaks fluent Annishnawbe Ojibway. It gets stranger and stranger.

BARB:

Why wouldn't she? She's been here over fifty years. Her and Mom used to rattle on for hours.

JANICE:

So what did she call me again?

BARB:

Wawasquaneh sim.

JANICE:

What does it mean?

BARB:

My little flower.

JANICE:

Amelia Earhart called me her little flower?

BARB:

No. That's what Mom used to call you when you were a little baby. My little flower. Times were poor, so your first bed was made from old pillowcases patterned with flowers. So Mom started calling you her little flower. Wawasquaneh sim.

JANICE:

That's sweet.

BARB:

Isn't it.

JANICE:

I like Amy.

BARB:
 I'm so happy.

JANICE:
 This has got to be the greatest story of the decade.

BARB:
 What is? That Mom called you her little flower? Talk
 about a slow news day.

JANICE:
 No. Amelia. Here, in Otter Lake.

BARB:
 Oh, but that's our story, the village's.

JANICE:
 I can't believe you won't let me tell anybody this. It's
 not fair.

BARB:
 She's a part of this community. This whole Reserve is
 like a family. You don't go telling secrets on family.

JANICE:
 And you consider her family?

BARB:
 She was one of Mom's best friends. And, remember,
 she's your Godmother.

JANICE:
 I know! My Godmother! Amelia Earhart is my
 Godmother. I gotta tell somebody. That is so cool.

 JANICE knocks over her bottle of beer, spilling it.

BARB:
 That wasn't.

JANICE:
    Barb, this is unbelievable.

BARB:
    What's so hard to believe?

JANICE:
    Barb, think about it. I was born here but I don't feel at home here and Amelia Earhart does. She's family and I'm not because the Children's Aid Society took me away. Doesn't all this seem a little weird to you?

BARB:
    After this many beers everything seems weird. *(testing JANICE)* Are you gonna tell on Amy?

JANICE:
    I don't think anyone would believe me.

BARB:
    Then Grace, you gotta problem.

JANICE:
    I really wish you wouldn't call me Grace.

BARB:
    Why not? It's your name.

JANICE:
    No, it's not. My name is Janice. I didn't know about "Grace" until six months ago. I don't feel comfortable being addressed that way. It's like somebody calling you Susan or Victoria all of a sudden. It doesn't feel right.

BARB:
    Fine, *Janice.*

JANICE:
    I've made you mad again, haven't I?

BARB:
You're just so white.

JANICE:
You make that sound so bad.

BARB:
It is. You're not white. You're Indian, Ojibway. Go look in a mirror.

JANICE:
I know what I am. I've spent most of my life trying to figure that out. I don't need you telling me what I am and am not.

BARB:
I don't have to tell you anything. Like I said, looking in the mirror will tell you everything.

JANICE:
I've been looking in the mirror for thirty-five years. Tell me what makes an Indian then, Barb? Come on tell me. What is an Indian? Is an Indian someone who drinks? Look, Barb, I'm drinking.

JANICE takes a swig of her beer.

BARB:
That's bullshit and you know it.

JANICE:
Do you speak this Ojibway language?

BARB:
Yeah, kinda.

JANICE:
Then if it's so important to you, teach it to me.

BARB:
> When?

JANICE:
> Right now. I'm pretty good with languages. What do
> you call this?

> *JANICE holds up a bottle of beer.*

BARB:
> You're crazy.

JANICE:
> No, I want to know. What do you call a bottle of beer?

BARB:
> It isn't that easy....

JANICE:
> If you try hard enough, anything can be easy. Beer!

BARB:
> Beer. Let's see. *(thinking)* Shinkopiiwaabo. That sounds
> like it.

JANICE:
> Shinki...Shinki....

BARB:
> Shinkopiiwaabo.

JANICE:
> Shinkopiiwaabo. Wine.

BARB:
> Um, wine is Zhoominaabo.

JANICE:
> Zhoominaabo. Shinkopiiwaabo and Zhoominaabo.
> Window.

BARB:
Waasechikan.

JANICE:
Waasechikan. How about that lake out there?

BARB:
Saakaikan. Is any of this sinking in?

JANICE:
Don't rush me. Saakaikan. So far so good. What's next?

BARB:
Ahneen, hello. Co-waabmen, I'll be seeing you.

JANICE:
Ahneen, co-waabmen. Next.

BARB:
Numbers. Want your numbers?

JANICE:
Shoot.

BARB:
Okay, repeat after me.

> *JANICE tries very hard to mimic each word.*

BARB:		JANICE:
One	...	Pashig
Two	...	Niish
Three	...	Nswi
Four	...	Niiwin
Five	...	Naanan
Six	...	Koodswaswi
Seven	...	Niizhwaaswi
Eight	...	Niizhwaaswa

> *JANICE stumbles over the Ojibway number eight.*

JANICE:
Nishwash.

BARB bursts out laughing.

JANICE:
What? What did I say?

BARB:
(through the laughter) Nishwash!

JANICE:
What?

BARB:
You said Nishwash. That means a guy's crotch.

JANICE:
Nishwash?!

JANICE bursts out laughing too.

JANICE:
Maybe I should wait till I'm sober.

BARB:
Oh, I wish the boys were here for that one. That was
funny.

JANICE:
Hey, maybe I can teach you something. I can speak
French fluently, some Italian, and I'm still pretty good
with Latin. A hold over from my school days.

BARB:
An Indian who speaks Italian and Latin. How do you
say, "Want another beer?" in Italian?

JANICE:
That would be, "Vuole un'altra birra?"

BARB:
Forget it. I won't even try that.

JANICE:
And the correct answer would be "Si, Certamente," certainly. Wanna learn some French?

BARB:
No thanks. Four years of high school French taught me all I'd need to know. Ou est la salle de bain? I figure with that under my belt, I can survive just about anything.

JANICE:
Then I guess I have nothing to teach you.

BARB is silent for a moment.

BARB:
You could do me a favour.

JANICE:
Me? What?

BARB:
You know about money, right? I mean you obviously aren't hurting….

JANICE:
Barb, are you hitting me up for a loan?

BARB:
Don't flatter yourself. It's all that money we got from the lottery Mom won.

JANICE:
If you want, I can set you up with some good investment consultants.

BARB:

You. Why don't you look after it for us?

JANICE:

It would be better if you had a professional….

BARB:

It would be better if we had family looking after family.

JANICE:

It would make me feel uncomfortable.

BARB:

And giving all our money to some white stranger will make me feel comfortable?

JANICE:

You asked for my opinion, I gave it.

BARB:

Never mind. I'm sorry I asked. This is not the kind of conversation you would hear on your typical Indian Reserve. Maybe we could start a whole new Reserve for people like you, where you could talk about investment counsellors, and jazz guitarists and Saabs and stuff.

JANICE:

Are you trying to hurt me?

BARB:

I can get a car out of a snow covered ditch. I can chop wood, clean a fish. Not much call for those talents in the big city, huh?

JANICE:

I guess Tonto would have to join me on that Reserve.

BARB:

No, Tonto's as Indian as they come. It has nothing to do with being adopted. It has to do with being taken away. Some are taken away but never leave. You had a whole family waiting to accept you and you ran. You took yourself away. That's the difference. And unfortunately, that's the truth of the matter.

JANICE:
For you. I have my own truth.

BARB:
Truth is truth. You're just playing lawyer again.

JANICE:
You wanna play lawyer? You wanna play fucking lawyer? Your honour, my client, one Janice Wirth was taken into custody by the Children's Aid Society in 1955 in the false belief that her mother, Anne Wabung was not maintaining a proper and adequate home environment for the infant. It appeared the father had abandoned the family when, in fact, the father had secretly enlisted in the army as a means of providing financial assistance for his family. Flash forward thirty-five years. After many years of soul searching and trepidation, my client seeks out her birth family, to put the final piece in the puzzle of her life together. Satisfied with what she's learned, she returns to the world in which she was raised. However, finding herself under severe emotional stress due to her visit, my client is unable to resume work. She decides to take two months off, to deal with the bouncing around in her head. She finally gets herself back together when she finds herself right back where she began. In the same kitchen, with the same people, with the same problems. That, your honour is our case.

Silence.

BARB:
Wow, you're good at that.

JANICE:
  It's the truth.

BARB:
  I guess this is what Mom meant when she said only drunks and children tell the truth.

JANICE:
  Maybe.

BARB:
  Mom had a lot of sayings like that.

JANICE:
  My Mother didn't.

BARB:
  No?

JANICE:
  She was quite practical, serious. She didn't have much use for cute little sayings. I wonder what I would be like if I had grown up here.

BARB:
  Probably fatter.

JANICE:
  Wonderful. When I was a little girl, I always dreamt my Mother was somebody like Pocahontas or Sacajewea. I used to read all about them. Did you know Sacajewea was a Shoshoni word meaning Bird Woman?

BARB:
  Binshii-kweh. That means Bird Woman in Annishnawbe, Ojibway.

JANICE:
  Binshii-kweh. I must remember that. I also used to dream I had a sister.

BARB:
But probably not like me.

JANICE:
I seem to remember canoes and buckskin. I don't remember why though.

BARB:
Couldn't have been me then. Never had a buckskin dress in my life. And I hate canoeing, my legs cramp.

JANICE:
I wonder if that's why I bought that white fur coat of mine, my heritage coming through.

BARB:
Doubt it. You're the only Indian I know who has one.

JANICE:
I wanted to belong here so bad. When I drove up that driveway, it seemed like I had prepared my whole life for that meeting. But from the moment I arrived, I knew I didn't belong. You didn't even like me.

BARB:
I didn't like you because I knew you were going to hurt Mom.

JANICE:
How could you know that?

BARB:
Easy. You weren't real to her. You couldn't possibly be everything she dreamed. Somewhere down the line, she would realize you weren't a dream, weren't perfect, and her world would come crashing down. And as usual, I would be there to cry with her. It wasn't you I didn't like, it was the bomb I knew was waiting to go off. I didn't personally start to dislike you until you walked out. The minute that door closed behind you, I

knew it was over. *(beat)* You killed her, you know? As sure as you put a gun against her head. She died because of you.

JANICE:
That's not fair.

BARB:
No, it's not, is it? I loved Mom, she loved you, and you killed her.

JANICE:
Quit saying that.

BARB:
When you left, you took her spirit, her will to live, with you. She was dead long before last Tuesday. It just took a while for her body to catch up. Drink up, Janice.

JANICE punches BARB. She goes flying across the room, creating a loud crash.

JANICE:
Don't you dare hang all of that on my head. If you want to hate me then hate me. But you have no god-damn right to blame me for Anne's death. I'm part of this whole fucking picture too.

TONTO and RODNEY come running in, alerted by the noise.

JANICE:
(yelling) Get out!

Startled, the boys do as they're told quickly. BARB picks herself up slowly.

JANICE:
I am so sorry for Anne's death, but I am not responsible for what happened to her. I can't be. I can't handle more guilt. Why do you think I didn't want to come

here? I've got scars of my own. I know I walked out of here, and I have to live with that fact. You don't think I realize that she's gone and that I'll never know what kind of woman she was or what could have happened between us? I grew up wanting to hate this woman, thinking my whole life was her fault. That's why I ran out of this house. I was all prepared to dislike and pity some old Indian woman that lost me because of alcohol. Instead I find this wonderful, sweet, caring woman that had her baby taken away by the system for no good reason. A baby she loved and fought to get back. I began to feel it all. I started to care, Barb, but I didn't want to care. If I care, I'll realize what I've lost.

BARB:
Mom always said you couldn't miss something you never had.

JANICE:
She was wrong.

BARB:
I guess. Grace, you're all I've got left.

JANICE:
I thought you didn't like me.

BARB:
My brother's dead, my father, my mother. I'm an orphan. I don't wanna be alone.

JANICE:
You've got Rodney.

BARB:
It's not the same.

JANICE:
No, I guess it isn't. I don't feel well.

BARB:
   Neither do I.

JANICE:
   Oh, your poor face. What did I do?

BARB:
   Not my face. My stomach.

JANICE:
   I thought I hit you in the face?

BARB:
   You did. I think. But my stomach…. Can you help me
   sit down?

JANICE:
   Okay.

   *JANICE puts her arm around BARB and helps her over
   to a chair. Once BARB is sitting, JANICE takes her arm
   away but BARB grabs it.*

BARB:
   Thank you.

   *BARB passes out, her arm knocking the birthday present
   onto the floor. JANICE goes to make her more comfortable.*

JANICE:
   Poor Barb. I'm so sorry for your face, Anne, everything.

   *JANICE trips over the present on the floor. Drunkenly she
   picks it up. Fighting tears, she opens the present, revealing a large dreamcatcher.*

JANICE:
   What the hell is this?

   She notices a tag attached. She struggles to read it.

102

JANICE:
"...Good dreams pass through the webbing, bad dreams are caught and dissolved by the early morning light. Usually given to newlyweds to hang over the window in their bedrooms or to the mother of a new born baby, to ensure her baby will only have pleasant dreams." ...new born baby....

JANICE starts to cry, slowly she lays her head down on the table and passes out. The men enter tentatively, checking out the territory. TONTO lifts JANICE's head, but it falls with a thud.

TONTO:
Normally that should hurt.

TONTO examines the present.

TONTO:
What's all this stuff? Nice Dreamcatcher. Do you mind telling me what's going on here?

RODNEY:
It worked.

TONTO:
What worked?

RODNEY:
The plan. Barb's plan. With a little coaching from yours truly.

TONTO:
Oh God, what have you two done this time?

RODNEY:
They needed to bond. And nobody bonds like a couple of drunks.

TONTO:

But it's a false bonding. Drunks will kill each other
over the last mouthful of booze. You're playing with
fire.

RODNEY:

Firewater?!

TONTO:

Damn it, Rodney, this is serious. Alcohol doesn't solve
problems, it creates them.

RODNEY:

I know, I know, but the system fucked them up royally.
Something equally screwy had to fuck them back down.
Fight fire with fire.

TONTO:

I used to work in a Detox Centre, you didn't. Two
wrongs don't make a right.

RODNEY approaches BARB.

RODNEY:

Look at her. Sleeping peacefully. She just got drunk
with her adopted sister for the first time. I'm sure
there's a country song in there somewhere.

TONTO:

Rodney, why did you do this?

RODNEY:

I told you....

TONTO:

Uh uh. You told me what you did, but not why. There's
something going on in that book-clogged head of
yours. Let me have a peak.

RODNEY:
Anne.

TONTO:
Yes?

RODNEY:
The car accident, when Paul died. She never blamed
me for that.

TONTO:
Why should she? Wasn't your fault.

RODNEY:
He was coming to pick me up at the bar. I phoned him,
remember? He wouldn't have been on that road if it
hadn't been for me. Half the village was giving me dirty
looks but, God bless her, she never thought a single
bad thing about me. What a woman.

TONTO:
And all this...?

RODNEY:
I took part of her family away. I had to return another
part. Barb planted the idea but I cultivated it.
Remember the stuff with the night-blindness?

TONTO:
Oh, Rodney, man....

RODNEY:
It's okay now. Really.

BARB moans and wakens.

BARB:
Rodney?

RODNEY:
    Right here, Barb.

BARB:
    I love my Mother.

RODNEY:
    I know you do, sweetie. And she loves you.

BARB:
    Put me in her bed. I want to sleep there.

RODNEY:
    Sure thing.

        *RODNEY helps the almost unconscious BARB toward the
        bedroom.*

TONTO:
    Okay genius, what do I do with this one?

RODNEY:
    Put her in Barb's room. And Tonto, better get some
    buckets out of the back room.

TONTO:
    Good idea. Oooh, are you gonna be in pain tomorrow,
    Kemosaabe.

Scene Three

The scene opens on a graveyard. All four enter the grounds. Again the women are leaning quite heavily on the men. BARB and JANICE are in pain.

BARB:
> *(squinting)* Rodney, do something about that sun, please?

JANICE:
> *(to TONTO)* Not so fast. Easy. Slow down. Never again.

BARB:
> Rodney, Rodney, if you love me, you'll kill me right now.

JANICE:
> I may never eat again.

RODNEY:
> Boy, I wish we had a camera.

> *They arrive at Anne's grave.*

TONTO:
> Here we are.

JANICE:
> So this is it.

TONTO:
> You sure you're up to this?

JANICE:
> No time like the present.

TONTO:
> Still, it is kinda tacky visiting your Mother's grave hung over.

RODNEY:
That's my Barb, tacky all the way.

BARB:
Okay, you guys, get away. Go wait at the car. This is daughter stuff.

RODNEY:
You sure? You look a little unsteady.

BARB:
It's okay. We'll be fine.

RODNEY:
We'll be over here, if you need help.

The men exit.

JANICE:
God, I feel awful. Maybe this wasn't such a good idea.

BARB:
Mom used to say "self-inflicted wounds don't count." Janice, hold me up.

JANICE:
I can barely hold myself up.

BARB:
Okay. I'm okay.

BARB walks to the tombstone.

BARB:
Mom, look who I brought. It's Gra.... It's Janice, Mom. You were right. She did come home again.

JANICE:
I don't know what to say, Barb.

BARB:

You'll think of something. I got to go. I'm not feeling well.

BARB hobbles away in obvious pain.

BARB:

(calling plaintively) Rodney!!

JANICE is left alone at Anne's grave.

JANICE:

Hello Anne. Wherever you are, I hope you're feeling better than I am. The last time you saw me, I was a mess. Confused. In great emotional pain. Now it's physical pain. I don't know which one is better. *(pause)* Yes I do. The physical pain will go away. The emotional pain will take longer. If at all. I'm sorry I left the way I did. It must have been a horrible Christmas for you. But you must understand I didn't walk out on you. I walked out on me. To everybody I was Grace, but to me I'm Janice. I don't know if I can ever be the Grace you wanted, or the Grace Barb wants. I don't know anything any more. I'm hungover. I've met Amelia Earhart. And I'm standing at your grave, a woman I barely got to know. What a town this Otter Lake of yours. I guess the reason I'm here is to seek forgiveness for the bad thoughts I had, about you. I couldn't help it. I needed a reason, some excuse for what happened to me, what I went through. You were all I had. Growing up in the home I did, looking the way I do, the schools I went to, the jokes I heard. I had to blame somebody. I feel so ashamed. You were so kind to me, so nice. And all I wanted was evidence, proof to justify my anger. And there you were, so sweet and accepting. My whole life fell away. Everything I had wanted to believe was gone because of you. That made me even more angry. I hate myself now. I'm tired of being angry. I'm tired of mistrusting you. I'm tired of everything. I just don't want to fight it any more. I'm sorry. You deserve better....

JANICE collapses. TONTO comes running up to her side.

TONTO:
  Yo, Janice, are you okay?

JANICE:
  I don't know any more.

TONTO:
  Know what?

JANICE:
  Anything.

TONTO:
  That's an awful lot to forget after one night of drinking. Trust me, you know everything you need to know.
  People may learn a few facts or stories over the years,
  but all the real important things in life we know at
  birth.

JANICE:
  I don't need grave-side therapy right now. You had it
  easy, you grew up here. You knew everything.

TONTO:
  That has nothing to do with it. Janice, have you ever
  heard of a bird called a cowbird? *(JANICE shakes her
  head)* Interesting bird the cowbird. They lay their eggs
  in other birds' nests then fly off.

JANICE:
  (sniffling) Cuckoos.

TONTO:
  What?

JANICE:
  Cuckoos. The English have a similar bird called a
  cuckoo.

TONTO:

Whatever. Anyway, the robins or starlings, whichever the nest belongs to, they raise the baby cowbird as a robin or a starling or whatever. But when it grows up, the cowbird is still a cowbird. It lays its eggs in another bird's nest just like any other cowbird. Somewhere, deep inside, it knew it was a cowbird. No matter how it was raised or what it was taught. What are you, robin or cowbird?

JANICE:

I don't know.

TONTO:

Well, let's go find out.

JANICE:

What do you think I've been trying to do all these years?

TONTO:

Yeah, but you've been doing it alone. 2, 3, 4, 8, 10, heads are better than one.

JANICE:

But it's not your problem.

TONTO:

I'm a cowbird too, remember. Let me help, okay?

Beat.

JANICE:

Why not?

TONTO:

Are you done here?

JANICE:

Not yet. Go ahead, I'll be down in a moment.

TONTO exits. Janice turns around and looks at the grave one last time. She sees a daisy growing off to the side. She picks it and gently places it against the headstone.

JANICE:

Co-waabmen, Mom, from your daughter, Grace.

JANICE walks towards the car exiting.

The lights go down.

THE END